ANIMALS
AROUND THE WORLD

Sarah Creese

make
believe
ideas

Amazing animals live everywhere,
with scales, wings and furry hair.
Look in the desert, the forest and sea,
but don't visit when it's time for tea!

Reading together

This book is an ideal first reader for your child, combining simple words and sentences with stunning colour photography of real-life animals. Here are some of the many ways you can help your child take those first steps in reading. Encourage your child to:

- Look at and explore the detail in the pictures.
- Sound out the letters in each word.
- Read and repeat each short sentence.

Look at the pictures

Make the most of each page by talking about the pictures and spotting key words. Here are some questions you can use to discuss each page as you go along:

- Why do you like this animal?
- What would it feel like to touch?
- Where does it live?
- Does it look cute or scary?

Look at rhymes

Some of the sentences in this book are simple rhymes. Encourage your child to recognise rhyming words. Try asking the following questions:

- What does this word say?
- Can you find a word that rhymes with it?

- Look at the ending of two words that rhyme. Are they spelled the same? For example, "found" and "ground", and "night" and "fight".

Test understanding

It is one thing to understand the meaning of individual words, but you need to check that your child understands the facts in the text.

- Play "spot the obvious mistake". Read the text as your child looks at the words with you, but make an obvious mistake to see if he or she catches it. Ask your child to correct you and provide the right word.
- After reading the facts, shut the book and make up questions to ask your child.
- Make statements about the animals and ask your child whether the statements are true or false.
- Provide your child with three answers to a question and ask him or her to pick the correct one.

Quiz pages

At the end of the book there is a simple quiz. Ask the questions and see if your child can remember the right answers from the text. If not, encourage him or her to look up the answers.

Animals around the world

Animals live all around the world.

They live in oceans, forests, deserts, mountains and rivers.

My fur is orange,
black and white.
Stripy patterns
hide me from sight.

Roar!

Did you know?

Tigers live in Asia. They can usually
be found in forests.

Tiger

Slow and silent,
I stalk my prey.
I can hunt at night,
or during the day.

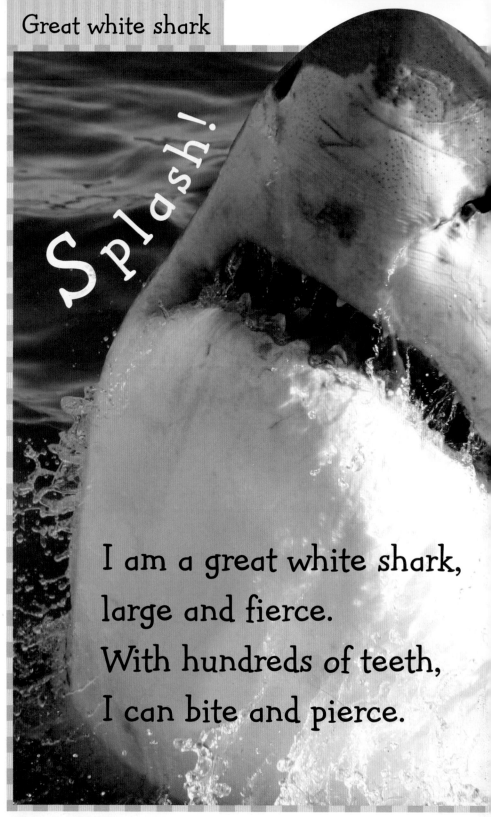

Splash!

I am a great white shark,
large and fierce.
With hundreds of teeth,
I can bite and pierce.

Did you know?

Great white sharks live in oceans all over the world.

shark teeth

I live in the desert.
I come out at night.
With pincers and stinger,
I'm armed for a fight.

Did you know?

Some scorpions can survive by
eating just one insect a year!

Snap!

I'm big and strong,
with furry brown hair.
I can run fast.
I'm a grizzly bear.

Grrrrr!

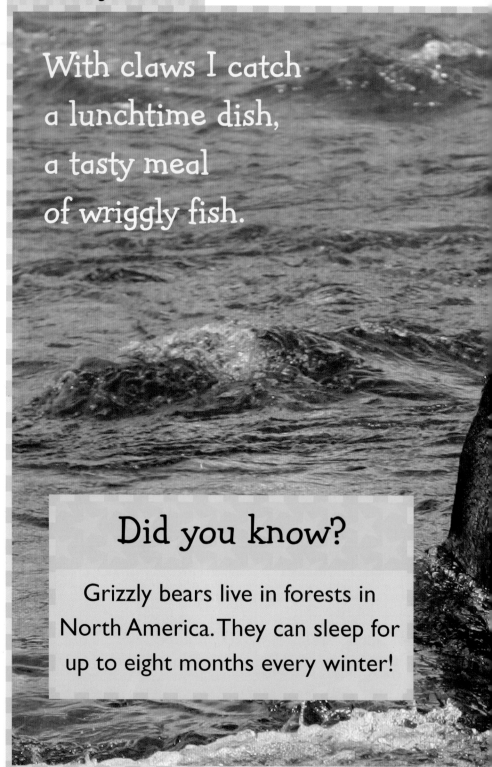

With claws I catch
a lunchtime dish,
a tasty meal
of wriggly fish.

Did you know?

Grizzly bears live in forests in
North America. They can sleep for
up to eight months every winter!

In rainforests and plains,
I can be found.
I can lift my body
high off the ground.

Did you know?

The king cobra hunts
other snakes in South Asia.

Hissss!

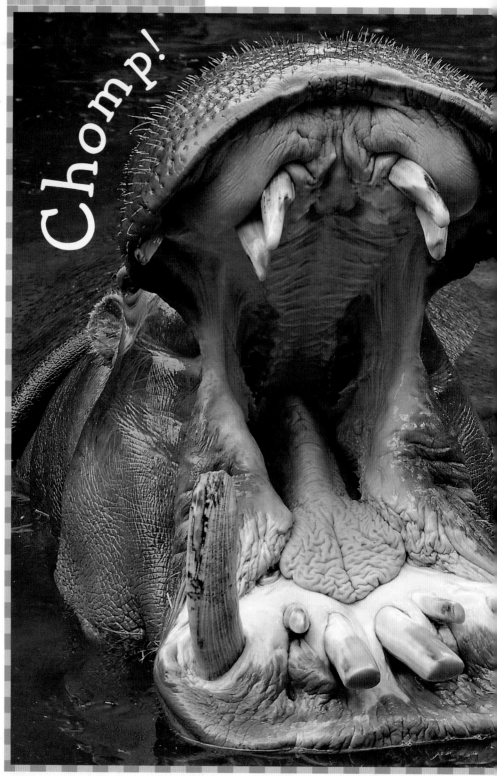

Chomp!

I have short legs.
I'm fat and wide.
When I open my mouth,
see my big teeth inside!

Did you know?

Hippos live in Africa.
They spend most of their day
in rivers and lakes.

I am an animal
with scaly skin.
In rivers and marshes
I hide and swim.

Beware!

Did you know?

Crocodiles can be found all over the world in rivers, lagoons, swamps and marshes.

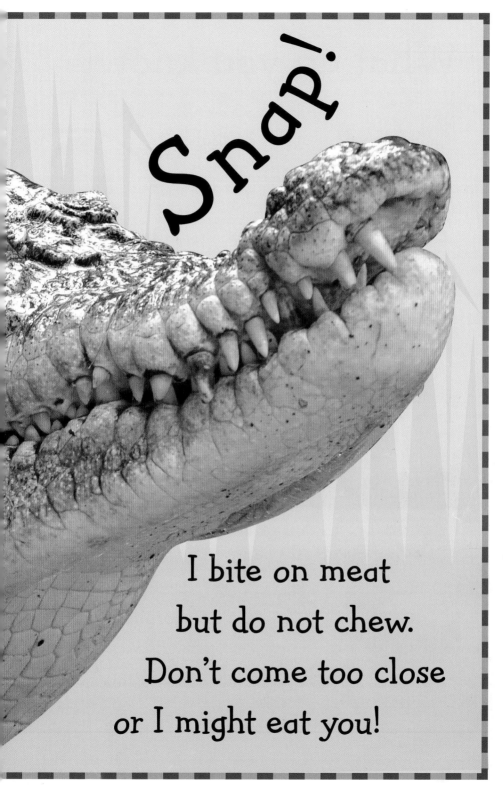

Snap!

I bite on meat
but do not chew.
Don't come too close
or I might eat you!

What do you know?

1. Which dangerous animal has hundreds of teeth?

2. Which fat animal has short legs?

3. Which animal can lift its body high off the ground?

4. Where in the world do hippos live?

5. What helps tigers to hide from sight?

6. What do grizzly bears like to eat?

7. Where do scorpions live?

8. Where do crocodiles live?

9. How long can grizzly bears sleep during the winter?

10. Where in the world do tigers live?

11. Where do hippos spend most of their day?

12. Which desert animals have pincers and stingers?

Answers

1. A great white shark. **2.** A hippopotamus. **3.** A king cobra. **4.** Hippos live in Africa. **5.** Their stripy patterns. **6.** They like to eat fish. **7.** Scorpions live in the desert. **8.** Crocodiles live in rivers, lagoons, swamps and marshes. **9.** Grizzly bears can sleep for up to eight months. **10.** Tigers live in Asia. **11.** Hippos spend most of their day in rivers and lakes. **12.** Scorpions have pincers and stingers.

Dictionary

forest

A forest is an area with lots of trees and plants.

scaly

Scaly skin is made up of small plates, which overlap each other like roof tiles.

stalk

To stalk another animal is to follow it closely and secretly.

pincer

A scorpion's pincer is a claw that it uses to catch food.

marsh

A marsh is land that floods with water all the time.

Key words

Here are some key words used in context.
Make simple sentences for the other
words in the border.

I **am** a scorpion.

My legs are short.

I **can** hunt during the
night or the day.

Grizzly bears **like**
to eat fish.

Crocodiles swim
in the water.